Garden to Plate

Contents   **Page**

written by Rosalind Hayhoe

Vegetables are delicious, and we should eat them every day because they contain vitamins and minerals that help us to grow and stay healthy. Vegetables like lettuce, tomatoes, peas and beans are easy to grow at home, and they taste even better if you have picked them fresh from your own garden.

Location, location

You don't need a large garden to grow some vegetables. What you do need is a sunny location, good soil and regular watering. Vegetables can be grown in the ground in your garden, or you can grow them in pots on your deck, patio or balcony. Spring is the best time to start growing vegetables because as the temperatures rise, the ground becomes warmer, and there are longer hours of sunshine to help plants grow.

Preparation

If you want to grow vegetables in the garden, choose a sunny spot with good soil. The ground shouldn't be too hard or too sandy. After measuring out the size you need for your garden, use a spade or a gardening fork to dig and turn the soil over until it is finely broken up, without any clumps.

It is a good idea to dig some compost into the soil. Compost is organic matter that is made from things like vegetable peelings, egg shells, dead leaves and grass clippings. It rots down and turns into food and soil for new plants to grow in. Compost helps crops grow because it supplies nutrients to plants and helps to loosen up soil so that it is easier to dig. You can buy compost in bags, or you can make your own compost at home in a large container in your garden. Composting is a great way to recycle your kitchen and garden waste.

compost bin

To grow plants in containers or pots, make sure they are large enough to allow the vegetables plenty of space to grow. Pour in the soil to just below the top of the pot. You can buy bags of special soil called Container or Potting Mix, which is ideal because it already has all the nutrients your plants need. Make sure that you put the pots in a warm sunny position to help the plants grow.

Planting seeds directly into the soil is the most economical way to grow vegetables.

Ideal plants to grow direct from seeds are: carrots, radishes, spinach, peas, beans and beetroot.

Follow these steps:

- make a row in the soil with your finger
- sprinkle seeds along the row
- cover with a fine layer of soil or compost
- water gently.

As long as your garden is in a warm place and you keep the soil moist, the seeds will germinate into small plants. It's a wise idea to stick a label with the vegetable's name into the soil, so that you remember what you planted in each row.

CAULIFLOWER

If you don't want to wait for seeds to germinate, you could use vegetable seedlings instead. Place these little plants into small holes you have dug in the soil, leaving enough space between the seedlings for them to grow larger. Carefully cover the roots of the plant with soil and sprinkle water over them. Some vegetables that grow well from seedlings are: tomatoes, broccoli, lettuce, cabbage, cucumber and peppers.

Watering

Be sure to apply sunscreen and wear a hat when you are gardening. If it is going to be a very hot day, try to work in your garden either early in the morning, or late in the afternoon when it isn't so hot. It is important to water your plants regularly. The best time of day to water them is in the morning before the temperature begins to rise. This gives them a good supply of water to last through the heat of the day. Pull out any weeds that start to grow around plants, so they are not crowding them or stealing nutrients they need from the soil. Weeding is easy when the ground is soft after rainfall, or after you have watered the garden.

Some plants like tomatoes, peas, and runner beans grow very tall and need to be tied up so that they don't fall over. Push three or four long sticks into the soil around each plant, being careful to avoid damaging the roots; tie the main branches of the plant to the sticks with some gardening twine or soft material. Now the vegetables can grow up high off the ground – they will be quicker to ripen and easier to pick.

Harvest time

After a few weeks of caring for your crops, it will be harvest time.
Check your garden every day, and pick the ripe vegetables to
encourage more to grow. Don't let cucumbers or zucchini get too
big – they taste better when they are small. You may need to use
a bucket to carry all the vegetables back to the kitchen!

You can try growing other types of plants, too. If you have a lot of room in your garden, try growing a melon or a giant pumpkin. Parsley, mint and basil are some herbs that are easy to grow in pots near your kitchen. Strawberries and blueberries grow easily too, and provide lots of sweet fruit. Flowers like sunflowers, daisies or marigolds look pretty in pots or planted around your vegetable garden.

Of course, the best thing about growing your own vegetables is eating them! Make sure you wash them well before you eat or cook them, and don't forget to share them with your friends! Eat and enjoy!